DATE DUE

PRIMARY SOURCES OF EVERYDAY LIFE IN COLONIAL AMERICA™

Money and Finance in Colonial America

Charlie Samuel

The Rosen Publishing Group's
PowerKids Press™
New York

Published in 2003 by The Rosen Publishing Group, Inc.
29 East 21st Street, New York, NY 10010

First Edition

Photo Credits: key: t: top, b: bottom, r: right, l: left
p.4 Peter Newark's American Pictures; p.6 Corbis/Bettmann; p.8tl Mary Evans Picture Library; p.8b Hulton Archive; p.11tr Peter Newark's American Pictures; p.11b National Park Service, Colonial National Historical Park, Yorktown, Virginia; p.12tl Hulton Archive; p.12b Corbis/Library of Congress; p.15tr British Museum; p.15br Bridgeman Art Library; p.15bl Christie's Images; p.16 Peter Newark's American Pictures; p.19cl & cr British Library; p.19tl Mary Evans Picture Library; p.20 Corbis/Lee Snider.

Library of Congress Cataloging-in-Publication Data

Samuel, Charlie.
  Money and finance in colonial America / Charlie Samuel.
      v. cm. — (Primary sources of everyday life in colonial America)
Includes bibliographical references and index.
Contents: Land of opportunity — Native American 'money' — Europe's merchant bankers — Colonial merchants — Bartering — Coins — Paper currency — Taxes — Early banks and bankers — Next steps for American finance.
  ISBN 0-8239-6602-X (library binding)
  1. Money—United States—History—Colonial period, ca. 1600–1775—Juvenile literature. 2. Finance—United States—History—Juvenile literature. [1. Money—United States—History—Colonial period, ca. 1600–1775. 2. Finance—United States—History.] I. Title. II. Series.
  E188 .S19 2003
  332'.0973'09032–dc21

                                        2002004837

Contents

▼ These Native Americans in Florida are collecting gold from a river. Stories about the wealth of native peoples were one of the reasons why Europeans were eager to explore North America.

Land of Opportunity

When Europeans began to hear stories about America at the end of the fifteenth century, the stories said that it was a rich land. People heard that there was gold in the ground and in the rivers. There was good land to farm, and there were animals to hunt for fur, and fish to catch for food. With such plentiful **resources**, America sounded like a place where it would be easy to live well and make money by trade.

Europeans soon began moving to America, where they started new communities called **colonies**. The Spanish started the first colonies in Mexico, the American Southwest, and Florida. The French had colonies in Canada and later in the Mississippi River valley. In North America the Dutch and the Swedish had small colonies on the East Coast at New Netherland and Delaware, but they were taken over by the English. By 1669, the English had a total of 13 colonies that stretched along the East Coast.

Native American "Money"

On the East Coast, the colonists met Native American peoples such as the Choctaw, Creek, Iroquois, and Wampanoag. Some native peoples did not trust the colonists, and attacked them. Other native peoples were more friendly. They showed the colonists how to grow American crops, and traded with them.

Native Americans traded using wampum, or shells that came from a kind of sea creature named the quahog. The shells were made into belts. In 1637, wampum became official money in Massachusetts. People even put wampum into the collection plate at church. Some people used wampum shells of poor quality, however. The shells broke easily. Wampum lost its value. By 1661, it was no longer used as money.

Europeans also traded with Native Americans by exchanging other goods for furs. Native Americans particularly valued copper and brass goods. They broke up brass kettles to make arrowheads and jewelry.

▶ This picture shows European traders smoking pipes to seal a deal with the Illinois Nation.

▼ This Native American is showing a piece of wampum to some men smoking a pipe beside a fire.

▼ This picture shows eighteenth-century French merchants gathered at a dock to welcome the latest cargo from New France, today called Canada.

▲ This seventeenth-century ship was owned by the Dutch West India Company, which ran trade between the Netherlands, the Caribbean, and North America.

Europe's Merchant Bankers

European **merchants** formed companies to fund early colonies. They got **charters** to start colonies in the hopes that they would be able to make money from trade. The Virginia Company funded the first English settlement at Jamestown in 1607, for example.

The merchants who formed the companies wanted to sell goods from America in Europe. To begin with, the most common American **exports** were animal furs, particularly beaver furs. They were valuable and easy to pack onto a ship. Dutch and French merchants were leaders of the fur trade. Merchants also hoped to sell colonists goods from Europe. In that way, the companies would profit from both exports and **imports**.

Colonies were risky, however. The Virginia Company went out of business in 1624, after bad harvests and disease killed nearly all of the settlers. The **investors** lost their money.

◄ *These ships from America are on the Thames River in London, the capital city of England.*

Colonial Merchants

Merchants in America often began work as **factors**, people who arranged cargoes for trading companies in England. They bought goods and saw that they were properly loaded onto a ship. In the southern colonies, the goods included tobacco, rice, and **indigo**. The colonies around Chesapeake Bay sent wheat and flour to Europe and the West Indies. In New England, to the north, fur, timber, and fish were important.

In the southern colonies, many merchants were also farmers. They sold the tobacco and rice they grew on large farms called **plantations**. Northern merchants traded a wider range of goods. They sometimes owned their own ships.

After 1651, merchants in the English colonies had to obey the Navigation Acts. These laws, passed by England, said that many goods from America had to be shipped to England on English ships. Colonial merchants felt that the laws prevented them from selling their goods to other customers who might pay more.

► *A price list from 1703 shows the cost of goods, including tools, corn, and tobacco. The prices are given in beaver skins, which were used to trade with Native Americans. Merchants could sell the beaver skins in Europe to make money.*

July 14th. 1703.
Prices of Goods

Supplied to the

Eastern Indians,

By the several Truckmasters ; and of the Peltry received
by the Truckmasters of the said *Indians*.

One yard Broad Cloth, *three* Beaver skins, *in season.*
One yard & half Gingerline, *one* Beaver skin, *in season.*
One yard Red or Blew Kersey, *two* Beaver skins, *in season.*
One yard good Duffels, *one* Beaver skin, *in season.*
One yard & half broad fine Cotton, *one* Beaver skin, *in season.*
Two yards of Cotton, *one* Beaver skin, *in season.*
One yard & half of half thicks, *one* Beaver skin, *in season.*
Five Pecks Indian Corn, *one* Beaver skin, *in season.*
Five Pecks Indian Meal, *one* Beaver skin, *in season.*
Four Pecks Pease, *one* Beaver skin, *in season.*
Two Pints of Powder, *one* Beaver skin, *in season.*
One Pint of Shot, *one* Beaver skin, *in season.*
Six Fathom of Tobacco, *one* Beaver skin, *in season.*
Forty Biskets, *one* Beaver skin, *in season.*
Ten Pound of Pork, *one* Beaver skin, *in season.*
Six Knives, *one* Beaver skin, *in season.*
Six Combes, *one* Beaver skin, *in season.*
Twenty Scaines Thread, *one* Beaver skin, *in season.*
One Hat, *two* Beaver skins, *in season.*
One Hat with Hatband, *three* Beaver skins, *in season.*
Two Pound of large Kettles, *one* Beaver skin, *in season.*
One Pound & half of small Kettles, *one* Beaver skin, *in season.*
One Shirt, *one* Beaver skin, *in season.*
One Shirt with Ruffels, *two* Beaver skins, *in season.*
Two Small Axes, *one* Beaver skin, *in season.*
Two Small Hoes, *one* Beaver skin, *in season.*
Three Dozen middling Hooks, *one* Beaver skin, *in season.*
One Sword Blade, *one & half* Beaver skin, *in season.*

*What shall be accounted in Value equal
One Beaver in season : Viz.*

One Otter skin in season, is one Beaver.

One Bear skin in season, is one Beaver.

Two Half skins in season, is one Beaver.

Four Pappcote skins in season, is one Beaver.

Two Foxes in season, is one Beaver.

Two Woodchocks in season, is one Beaver.

Four Martins in season, is one Beaver.

Eight Mincks in season, is one Beaver.

Five Pounds of Feathers, is one Beaver.

Four Raccoones in season, is one Beaver.

Four Sell skins large, is one Beaver.

One Moose Hide, is two Beavers.

One Pound of Castorum, is one Beaver.

▼ *This picture shows a factor watching barrels of tobacco being loaded onto a ship in Jamestown, Virginia.*

◄ Mills like this one ground grain into flour. Colonists paid the miller by giving him a share of the flour and meal in return for his work.

▼ Europeans and Native Americans barter for goods. In the early days of the colonies, the two peoples often traded by exchanging goods. Native Americans had always traded with each other in this way.

Bartering

There was little money in the early colonies. It was difficult to buy things. Only a few people had coins or banknotes. There was no single **currency** that was used everywhere. Money from one colony was no good in another. Colonial money was also useless for trading with Native Americans.

Instead of using money, people had to **barter** for what they wanted. They exchanged goods for other goods. To buy flour, for example, a colonist might give the **miller** a piece of cloth or some jars of honey. Everyone could do what they were good at, such as growing food or making clothes. They could then trade what they made or grew for other things that they needed. Often they kept a record of their deals and settled them all at once every six months.

Women were very important in the barter system. They made many of the items that people wanted. It was women, not men, who wove cloth and grew vegetables in the garden.

Coins

In the 1600s, there were very few coins in America. In Canada, the French used the silver coin called the *petit ecu* or the gold coin called the *louis d'or*. Dutch colonists used the *gulden*. European coins were used in ports where there was a lot of trade.

The English government prevented its colonies from making their own coins. In 1652, however, the Massachusetts Bay Colony broke the law and started a **mint** in Boston. In 1684, however, when Massachusetts became a **royal colony**, the English ordered the mint to close.

The most common coin in America was the silver "piece of eight," or Spanish dollar. It was made by the Spanish, who had supplies of silver in Mexico and Peru. By 1750, about half the coins in America were pieces of eight. They could be used throughout the colonies.

Unlike coins today, the old coins contained real gold and silver. The metals were so valuable that people cut little pieces off coins, to steal the metal.

► This pine tree shilling was minted in Massachusetts after 1652. Other shilling coins made in the colony had willow trees and oak trees stamped on them.

► This gold louis d'or was minted in France in 1640. The coins were used in the colonies until the eighteenth century.

◄ This picture shows merchants doing business at the docks in Manhattan in the middle of the eighteenth century. In busy ports some people used foreign coins that were brought by traders and sailors.

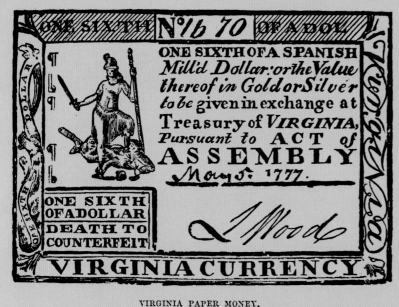

VIRGINIA PAPER MONEY.

◄ *This banknote was issued by Virginia in 1777. It is worth one-sixth of a Spanish dollar. It warns that death is the punishment to anyone trying to counterfeit, or make a copy of the money for themselves.*

► *This note was used to pay soldiers in the American Revolution in 1775.*

AMERICAN BILL OF CREDIT (1775).

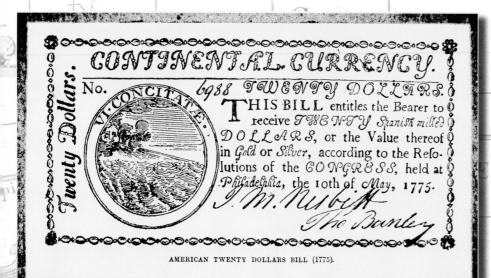

AMERICAN TWENTY DOLLARS BILL (1775).

◄ *This bill was issued by the Second Continental Congress that ran the United States in 1775. There were so many of the Continental bills that they were not worth very much.*

Paper Currency

It was easier for colonies to issue paper money than to issue coins. Making coins required gold or silver. Making paper money required only paper, which itself had no value. The French issued paper money in Canada in 1680. The first English colony to make paper money was Massachusetts, in 1690. South Carolina followed in 1703. The English colonies used paper money to pay soldiers who helped them to fight against the French in Canada.

The first paper money was like a written promise. It stated that the person who had the piece of paper would be paid a certain amount of something else, such as coins or goods, when such things were available.

Because paper money had no value of its own, many people refused to accept it as money. Colonies included seals and signatures on their money to show that it was genuine, so that people would accept it. Any person caught trying to copy money was punished by death.

Taxes

In the 1700s, people in the colonies paid taxes to the British government. The taxes paid for the costs of the colony, such as the wages of officials and the upkeep of roads.

Different types of taxes were charged in different colonies. Poll taxes charged a set amount to all adult males. Land taxes were based either on how much land a man owned, or on the value of what the land produced. Faculty taxes were based on a man's job and income. There was also a sales tax on certain goods. Before money became common, taxes were paid in goods such as tobacco or furs.

In 1765, the Stamp Act placed taxes on special paper used for newspapers and legal documents. The new taxes had not been approved by the colonial **assemblies**, as taxes usually were. Americans did not have any members in the British parliament. Unless they had a say in the government, they believed they should not pay taxes to it.

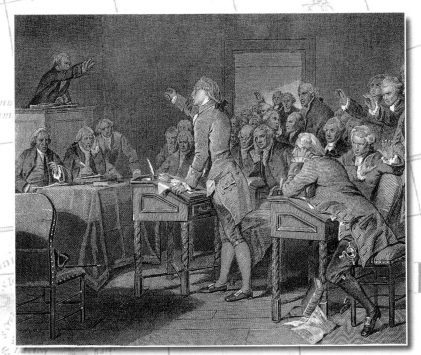

◄ In this picture, a politician named Patrick Henry protests the British taxes at a meeting of the assembly of Virginia.

► This register was used by a tax collector in the eighteenth century to list all the taxes that people had paid.

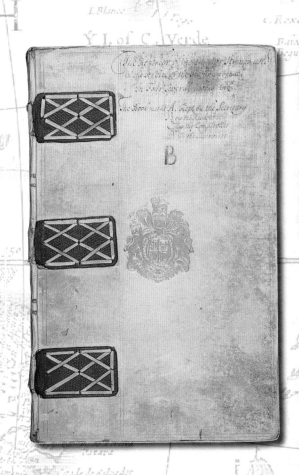

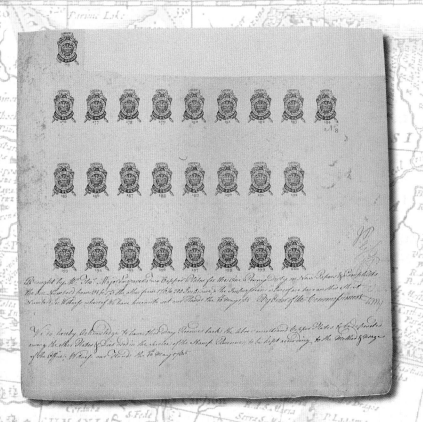

◄ These stamps had to be fixed to all American newspapers. When the British passed the Stamp Act to tax newspapers and other printed material, the colonists protested and had the tax removed.

◄ Mills such as this one, on Cape Cod in Massachusetts, sometimes acted as banks. Millers looked after people's money.

▼ The First Bank of the United States, in Philadelphia, was founded by Alexander Hamilton in 1791. Hamilton created a banking system for the new country.

Early Banks and Bankers

There were few real banks in the colonies. In some communities, however, the miller acted as a kind of banker. The miller was the most important businessman in the community. He looked after people's money and made loans.

In the early 1600s, Dutch settlers set up banks in New Netherland. The Bank of Amsterdam was a safe place to store coins, wampum, or other valuable goods. The British took over New Netherland in 1664, and renamed it New York. The Dutch banks closed.

In 1681, another bank opened in the colonies in Boston, Massachusetts. It was called The Fund. The Fund could make loans so that people could buy goods or real estate. A borrower paid back the loan with a sum of **interest**. By 1740, there were also banks in New Hampshire and Rhode Island.

Many colonial banks were set up by private individuals with their own money. Some were also set up with money from the government.

Next Steps for American Finance

From 1765 to 1774, the British placed a series of taxes on the colonies. American anger about the taxes and about British control of trade were important reasons for the outbreak of the American Revolution in 1776. Seven years later the new United States won the war.

The United States needed to create their own system of money, banks, and taxes. The war had been expensive, and the government was in **debt**. The man who did most work to shape the American economy was Alexander Hamilton, who became treasury secretary in 1789.

Hamilton said that the government would pay back the people who had loaned it money to fight the war. This was a sign that the country was a good place to invest money. In 1791, Hamilton started the Bank of the United States. In 1792, the United States opened a mint in Philadelphia, Pennsylvania, and began to make coins, including the dime and the dollar.

Glossary

assemblies (uh-SEM-bleez) Groups of people who meet to advise a government.

barter (BAR-tur) To trade.

charters (CHAR-turz) Written documents that allow an area of land to be used but not owned.

colonies (KAH-luh-neez) New places where people live but are still ruled by their old country's leaders.

currency (KUR-en-see) Something that can be used to pay for goods.

debt (DEHT) To owe other people money.

exports (EK-sports) Goods sold by one country to another.

factors (FAK-terz) Colonial merchants who set up deals on behalf of large companies.

imports (IM-ports) Goods brought into one country from another.

indigo (IN-dih-go) A blue dye from the indigo plant that was used to color cloth and other items.

interest (IN-ter-est) The extra cost that someone pays in order to borrow money.

investors (in-VES-turz) People who give money for something that they hope will bring them more money later.

merchants (MUR-chints) People who buy and sell goods.

miller (MIL-ler) A person who works in, operates, or owns a mill for grinding grain.

mint (MINT) A place where a country's money is made.

plantations (plan-TAY-shunz) Very large farms where crops such as tobacco and cotton were grown.

resources (REE-sors-ez) Things that occur in nature that can be used or sold, such as gold, coal, or wood.

royal colony (ROY-ul KAH-luh-nee) A colony whose rules were made by England.

Index

Primary Sources

Page 4. This picture of Native Americans in Florida was drawn in the sixteenth century by a Spanish colonist. **Page 7 (top).** This picture of the Illinois Nation trading with colonists was drawn by Nicholas de Fer in 1705 as part of a map he drew of the Western Hemisphere. **Page 7 (bottom).** This image of Native Americans is a lithograph. **Page 8 (top left).** This engraving from the 1600s shows a Dutch merchant ship. **Page 8 (top right).** This painting of French traders dates from the eighteenth century. **Page 8 (bottom).** The Tower of London stands at left of this view of the Thames River in the eighteenth century. **Page 11 (top).** This price list was printed on July 14, 1703. **Page 12 (top).** This engraving of a water mill was made in the eighteenth century. **Page 12 (bottom).** *Trading With Indians* was drawn by Theodor de Bry in 1634. **Page 15 (top).** This pine tree shilling was minted in Massachusetts. All pine tree shillings were dated 1652, though they continued to mint the coins through 1684. The Americans did this to try to make the English believe new coins were not still being made. **Page 15 (bottom).** The portrait on this gold louis d'or shows King Louis XIII of France. The coin was minted in France in 1640. **Page 16 (top).** This bill was worth one-sixth of a dollar. It was printed in Virginia in 1777. It has a serial number and is signed to make it more difficult to copy. **Page 16 (center right).** This bill was issued on August 18, 1775, to pay troops during the American Revolution. **Page 16 (bottom).** This 20-dollar bill was number 6988 issued by the Continental Congress in Philadelphia in 1775. **Page 19 (top).** The engraving of Patrick Henry shows an incident that happened in 1765. **Page 19 (center right).** This register was used by a colonial official in 1765. **Page 19 (bottom).** These numbered stamps were to be used to show that people had paid taxes to print newspapers and other documents. **Page 20 (top).** Dexter's Mill still stands in Cape Cod, Massachusetts. **Page 20 (bottom).** The First Bank of the United States, founded in 1791 in Philadelphia, Pennsylvania.

Web Sites

Due to the changing nature of Internet links, PowerKids Press has developed an online list of Web sites related to the subject of this book. This site is updated regularly. Please use this link to access the list: www.powerkidslinks.com/pselca/mfca.